GIVING: GOD'S
WAY

GIVING

God's Way

Way

John F.
MacArthur, Jr.

TYNDALE HOUSE
PUBLISHERS, INC.
WHEATON, ILLINOIS

To my good friend
and very special servant of God
EARL RADMACHER
who challenged and encouraged me
to think this subject through
and then make it available
to others.

Library of Congress Catalog Number 77-93748
ISBN 0-8423-1034-7
Copyright © 1978 by Tyndale House Publishers, Inc., Wheaton,
        Illinois 60187
Second Printing, December, 1978.
Printed in the United States of America.

CONTENTS

CHAPTER ONE   7
Holy Persuasion or High Pressure?

CHAPTER TWO   17
"The Silver Is Mine"

CHAPTER THREE   49
"Will a Man Rob God?"

CHAPTER FOUR   75
"As God Hath Prospered Him"

CONCLUSION   102

CHAPTER ONE
Holy Persuasion or High Pressure?

IF YOU are like most Christians, you have probably at one time or another deliberately avoided facing up to what the Scriptures say about giving. Perhaps the subject somewhat intimidated you into feeling guilty, or maybe you just found it incredibly dull. Perhaps when you knew the pastor was going to talk on giving, you decided it had been too long since you had visited Aunt Martha or you quickly volunteered to help with the nursery.

Granted, giving is not the most popular topic in Christian circles, but it is one of the most essential. And ignoring a responsibility doesn't negate it or even minimize it. But it does rob you of the joy of obedience.

There are many commands in the Word of God that are especially emphasized in terms of the blessing that accompanies them. Giving is one such command. Biblical teaching on this topic is a major part of the revelation of God, and so it must be important.

As the Apostle Paul was able to say to the Ephesian elders, so I want to be able to say to you that "I have not shunned to declare unto you all the counsel of God" (Acts 20:27, KJV). (But not in this one book!) Not to declare to you the principles of giving would rob you of blessing, and cause me to fall short of my responsibility.

I think it is important for us to put this in perspective because most Christians have been seriously done in on the teaching of giving. We are being pressured by the world to spend our money stupidly. And not only that, but we're often bombarded by Christians to spend it just as stupidly.

Let's face it—we really have a financial crisis in the church. We are often victimized by slick campaigning on the part of Christian organizations that are trying to loosen up our Christian bucks. If you've been a Christian any length of time and have gotten on any of the "Christian" mailing lists, you know what comes appealing for your Christian money. There seems to be no end to the number of people and organizations who want a donation. Some radio evangelists with a half-hour program spend twenty-five minutes asking for money and five minutes telling you what they will do with it. Christian bookstores offer us millions of dollars' worth of records, "holy hardware," and other "sanctified stuff."

As pastor of a church, I realize it's very urgent that Christians understand what God says about how they give their money, because we're being bombarded by Madison Avenue. Christian organizations hire admen to get your money out of your pocket. These people are not babes in the woods; they're experts in persuasion, or actually manipulation. When you get an appeal letter from a Christian organization, it may not have been written by anyone in that organization. It may have been written by a professional ad agency (at considerable expense—but it's worth it; God expects RESULTS).

When you see a TV offer for a bicentennial Bible, or a plot in Jerusalem, or a Jesus necklace, or a magic-charm knickknack with a Scripture verse on it, or a cross you can dangle, they know what they're doing. This is the super-sell, the hard-sell, the campaign-sell. The church is being pushed into a Madison Avenue mold. Now don't get me wrong. Many Christian organizations are good, and you ought to give money to them. But I want you to realize that some appeals do use questionable approaches.

We sometimes feel, in fact, like we're drowning in a flood of giving gimmicks, church stewardship drives, and budget promotions, *ad infinitum*, *ad nauseum*. We've all been victimized by this at one time or another.

Voltaire, the atheist, once remarked that Protestantism is merely a less expensive substitute for Catholicism. Sometimes I wonder.

Lukas Vischer commented on Voltaire's feeling by saying: "The French philosopher Voltaire was highly critical of the Roman Church for what he felt were its excesses and its avaricious demands. But he was even more critical of the Protestant churches for allowing themselves to be used as havens for those whose religious convictions were determined by the desire primarily to keep more of their money for themselves."

But in our time, the effort is on to loosen the Protestant purse strings.

In the eyes of some people, Christian financial appeals are nothing more than exploitation. For the pastor, there's a stream of literature telling how to increase the church budget. I read a book not long ago on how to develop a tithing church. It talked about slick ideas such as loyalty week and knock-on-every-door week, plus how to have a pledge system, how to canvass a neighborhood (for donations), how to motivate people to give, how to make them feel guilty and transfer their guilt into donations, etc. Or if you really get desperate, you can hire out-of-town experts who will come in and raise the money for you (for a piece of the action, of course). Several organizations exist in America to publish material you can post around your church to stimulate people to give money.

I'm not against stimulating Christians to give money. I'm just against doing it in an unbiblical way. I might illustrate the principle from another area. The evangelism campaign in one church involved hiding several footballs in the homes of unsaved families. If church members going door-to-door happened to come across an unsaved family with one of the footballs, they won a jacket. Well, I'm not against evangelism, but I'm sure that is not the biblical plan. How in the world would an unregenerate family ever understand Christians coming to them on the pretense of evangelism when it appears all they want is a jacket? So in giving, the end does not justify the means.

There are so many clever admen putting together these things, so many hucksters on TV and radio hounding you for money, that you feel as though you're being followed twenty-four hours a day by persistent super-salesmen.

Of course, you're also pressured by the unstable economic situation — "If you don't have the equivalent of six months' income stashed away, your future spells Trouble with a capital T," banks and other savings institutions insist. What happened to God? The Bible teaches saving, but you can become paranoid about this.

You're trapped between investing your money with God and being sure you can take care of your family's present and future needs. In the face of all this, you try being responsive to the Holy Spirit as He leads and guides you, believing He will not take you into financial failure.

It's sad that some churches' and Christian organizations' financial procedures are so distasteful. There are some churches, for example, where success is measured by the size of the offering. Prayer requests are often given in terms of monies needed. They might as well put big dollar signs on their church sign. THE FIR$T CHURCH OF CHRI$T.

In such churches no opportunity is ever lost for making appeals, and every possible approach and gimmick is used to make those appeals effective. Whenever large crowds gather for any meeting of any kind with any purpose in mind, the church seizes the opportunity to make money by taking a hopefully large offering. Some churches venture into the area of business, marketing tapes, books, etc., at a profit.

Some in the church fall into the danger of partiality to the rich. I would have to say that it is true that in many (though not all) churches the wealthiest people dictate theology and policies. Some of you have seen this happening. John Murray has said, "Perhaps few weaknesses have marred the integrity of the church more than the partiality shown to the rich. The church has compromised with their vices because it has feared the loss of their patronage. Its voice has been silenced by respect of persons, and dis-

cipline has been sacrificed in defer-
ence to worldly prestige."[1]

"My brethren, do not hold your
faith in our glorious Lord Jesus Christ
with an attitude of personal favoritism. For if a man comes into your as-
sembly with a gold ring and dressed in
fine clothes, and there also comes in a
poor man in dirty clothes, and you
pay special attention to the one who is
wearing the fine clothes, and say, 'You
sit here in a good place,' and you say
to the poor man, 'You stand over
there, or sit down by my footstool,'
have you not made distinctions among
yourselves, and become judges with
evil motives?" (James 2:1-4, NASB).

There's no place for partiality in the
church of Christ. Favoritism and love
are archenemies.

Other churches wield spiritual fear
in an attempt to pressure people into
giving. This is wrong. The right thing
to do is to teach the truths of the
Word of God, and then leave it to the
Spirit of God to generate the response. Instead of using gimmicks, we
are to declare the Word of God, as-
suming the Spirit of God will produce
in lives the kind of giving compatible
with biblical instruction.

[1] John Murray, *Principles of Conduct* (Grand Rapids:
William B. Eerdmans Publishing Co., 1957), p. 90.

Be sure to give intelligently. Giving is not necessarily "spiritual." We must do all we can to be wise stewards. On occasion people in my church have said, "Pastor, I just sent x number of dollars to So-and-so." And I may have to say, "Did you know that he teaches heresy, or he left his wife six months ago and now . . ." "But he said in such and such a letter . . ." But who wrote the letter and what was that letter designed to do? Examine the situation a little bit. Check out the individual or his organization before you get out your checkbook. God does not want His people to be duped.

To what should you have a giving response? Pledge systems? Faith-promise cards? Tithing? Professional fund-raising? "Christian hucksters" who hustle your bucks on radio and television?

Remember, giving is never to be by coercion, never by crafty fund-raising, never by compulsion or manipulation. Any gimmick is offensive to God. "Let each one do just as he has purposed in his heart; not grudgingly or under compulsion, for God loves a cheerful giver" (2 Corinthians 9:7, NASB).

Some churches feel tithing is the best way to motivate their people to give as they should. They may even agree that tithing is not actually taught in the New Testament (that is, that it was an Old Testament program not reiterated in the New Testament), and yet feel they must push tithing because they are afraid that if they don't, they won't get enough in the offering to keep the church operating.

Someone told me recently that if everybody in Christian churches in the United States were reduced to welfare income and all gave 10 percent, the church would nearly double its giving. Some pastors read that and say, "Wow! If I can just get our members to tithe, we've got it made!" But the thing we must keep in mind is that God doesn't want us to give "under compulsion." He wants "cheerful givers."

So when we talk about giving in the Christian church today, we see both exploitation and neglect. On the one hand, Christians are being robbed blind through high-pressure advertising. On the other, some believers are robbing God because they have no understanding of what God expects of their giving.

I trust and pray that this book will help some of God's people to gain clear knowledge of God's will for their giving. In view of that, I would encourage you to study for yourself the Scriptures discussed in this book.

CHAPTER TWO
"The Silver Is Mine"

N ARTICLE
I read recently claimed that you (and
I) spend 50 percent of your time
thinking about money — how to get it,
how to spend it, how to save it, how
much you need to pay for this and
that. Regardless of the accuracy of
that particular percentage, money is
on your mind a great deal.

The Bible has much to say about finances. God puts great stress on the
way you handle your dollars and
dimes. This is a key area of the Chris-

tian's life, one that if not in harmony with the Word of God causes severe problems. Usually when I preach about this subject, some Christians assume that I'm saying this in order to get a bigger offering or to get a big check from the pastors who bribed me to psych up their people. Wrong!

I sincerely believe that you must learn to glorify God with your money. Your financial dealings are probably the most abused area in your life. God wants glory out of your money, and Satan wants you to misuse it — who will you follow? The sad part of it is that most Christians don't even know how God wants them to use their cash. So they walk in spiritual poverty because of their ignorance.

As a Christian, you continually face money issues — how you feel about it, how you earn it, how you spend it, how you give it.

If you don't really know what God expects of you in this regard, you can't possibly experience genuine success.

In a sense, money is a good barometer of your spirituality, because the way you handle your money is an indication of your performance as a Christian steward. You deal with money constantly. You pay bills; you write checks; you receive paychecks;

you make bank deposits; you buy this; you put change in that. Money is a constant reality, and the stewardship of money is a critical area of life about which the Bible has much to say.

I have been very concerned in recent days about many of the things that have been going on in our world — inflation and various other economic crises, the problem of supplying food for the future, rising fuel costs, etc. All of these involve financial needs. And each of us has his own money tangles to tackle.

I believe the believer has a financial responsibility. There is a biblical pattern for the believer's stewardship of his money. This has a tremendous bearing on your spiritual life and fruitfulness.

A few months ago I heard a commentator say, "Preachers are the poorest credit risks in the United States. Credit bureaus substantiate this." If this is true, it is a tremendous blight on Christianity, because the Bible is extremely clear about the believer's financial responsibility. Several weeks before this writing, a man came to me and said, "I am a new Christian, and I have no idea what God requires of me financially. Could you teach me on that subject?" A woman came to me recently and said, "I have many questions about what I should do in the area of financial planning as a Christian." The Word of God is not vague about this subject, and you shouldn't be either. As in all areas of life, your money habits should demonstrate a stability and self-control not available to unbelievers.

Money morality. When we talk about money, we're talking about life, in a sense, because money is so central to our everyday living. Money is itself amoral; that is, it's not good or evil, but can be used for good or evil. Money corrupts, some say. And it's true that some rich, no matter how much they have, always want more. But aren't there greedy poor as well? It's not money that is the real problem, but people's attitude toward it.

Some feel that it is wrong for a Christian to have more money than is necessary for bare necessities. They advocate a kind of a Christian communism, on the basis of Acts 2. They claim that since believers had all things in common in the early church, therefore all Christians should get into some kind of community thing where they give everything to a common fund and dole it out according to need. After all, the Christian has no right to possess money, they say.

What does the Bible teach about all this? First of all, all money belongs to God. " 'The silver is Mine, and the gold is Mine,' declares the Lord of hosts" (Haggai 2:8, NASB). God was talking about all the nations of the world here. All the gold and silver in the world is God's. Deuteronomy 8:18 (NASB) adds, "But you shall remember the Lord your God, for it is He who is giving you power to make wealth." Notice: all money is God's; God grants to men the ability to earn that which is His — wealth, money.

1 Corinthians 4:7 (NASB) asks us, "And what do you have that you did not receive?" This is another way of saying that money (one application of this verse) is God's, but He entrusts it to you. So it is not assumed in the Bible that it is wrong to have money, but rather that God allows men to make money. Money is one of God's gifts to you.

Sadly, God's gifts, intended for man's good, are generally perverted into evil. Take, for example, God's gift of nature. Man takes the things he has learned from nature (we call this knowledge "science") and invents bombs which kill, machines which pollute, etc. (Of course, man also uses his knowledge for good at times, but the overriding characteristic of man is depravity.)

Or consider sex, God's idea for the pleasure and reproduction of man. It's good, and marriage is honorable, says Hebrews 13:4. The marriage bed is to be undefiled, but man perverts that. Food is a gift from God, one of many to "be received with thanksgiving" (1 Timothy 4:4, KJV). But man turns it into gluttony.

Man has a way of twisting all of God's good gifts (and He gives no other kind), including money. In 1 Timothy 6:17 (KJV), a passage talking about material riches, we read that God "giveth us richly all things to enjoy." God is no cosmic killjoy. God is not some browbeating kind of ogre who wants to keep everybody in pain and misery. God, the possessor of all monies, is willing to grant some to you. Job, Abraham, Isaac, and Jacob were extremely wealthy because God prospered them. Isaiah 2:7 (KJV) says of Israel, "Their land also is full of silver and gold, neither is there any end of their treasures." God is not selfish — He allows you to have money to use for His glory.

If I were an executive in a corporation and handled company funds like I sometimes handle God's money, I'd go to jail for embezzlement. That's something to think about. God holds me (and you) responsible for the way

I handle His money, and I must not take that responsibility lightly.

If your employer came to you and said, "Hey, here's $100. I want you to spend it carefully and wisely to purchase some things we need. Let me know how you used it." Boy, I'm telling you you'd take care of that hundred bucks. You'd come back and you'd say, "Well, I got this and this for the office, and I got thus and so that we needed, and I got the best price."

Do you ever act as though the money in your pocket is your own and you have no obligation to anybody? Whose is it really? It's God's, and if you must give an account to your employer, how much more of an account should you give to God? You must answer to God.

Money can be a blessing or a curse. The key is your attitude toward it. You always hear people say, "Well, if I had a million dollars I'd . . ." Maybe, maybe not. The question is not what you would do with a million dollars, but what are you doing with the ten in your pocket? You might think that if your ship came in, you would support a missionary or whatever. But what are you doing with the tenspot in your wallet? Or the dollar? Ecclesiastes 5:10, 11 (NASB) warns: "He who loves money will not be satisfied with

23

money . . . When good things increase, those who consume them increase." The more you have, the more
stores you go to and the more you
buy. It doesn't have to be that way,
but it usually is. One free translation
might say, "The only advantage to
money is to watch it slip through your
fingers. The more you have, the more
it goes."

Jesus said, "He who is faithful in a
very little thing is faithful also in
much; and he who is unrighteous in a
very little thing is unrighteous also in
much" (Luke 16:10, NASB). The con-
text of that statement is a discussion
about money.

No, it is not a question of having
more and doing more with it; it's just
a question of what you're doing with
what you have. Riches can obstruct
spirituality. Jesus said in Matthew
10:23 (KJV), "How hardly shall they
that have riches enter into the kingdom of God." How hardly!

Love of money. How do we regard
money? Well, let me tell you the
wrong way to regard it, and that is to
love it. The Apostle Paul said in
1 Timothy 6:10 (NASB), "The love of
money is a root of all sorts of evil."

It's not an easy thing to avoid loving
money. It's around us all the time.

Money is such a powerful and constant part of our lives. In normal circumstances, we are never away from money matters. It's almost always part of our doings.

Since we are not to love money, it follows that we're not to trust in it. In fact, to trust in money is idolatry, one of God's most serious charges against anyone. The Apostle Paul advised Timothy to "instruct those who are rich in this present world not to be conceited or to fix their hope on the uncertainty of riches, but on God" (1 Timothy 6:17, NASB).

Even if you derive your sense of security from money you say God provided for you, that's still idolatry. "You cannot serve God and mammon — riches" (Matthew 6:24, NASB).

"The love of money is a root of all sorts of evil." It's not money, but the love of it that is the problem. You can have a lot of it and not love it, and you can have none of it and love it. It's the love of money, not money, that disgusts God. When you derive your sense of security from your money rather than from your God, you're trapped in idolatry. God or money — choose your master.

"But godliness with contentment is great gain" (1 Timothy 6:6, KJV).

Godliness and contentment go together. When you're happy with what
you have, that really fits in with being
a godly person. "For we brought nothing into this world, and it is certain we
can carry nothing out. And having
food and raiment, let us be therewith
content" (vv. 7, 8). "Be content with
such things as ye have" (Hebrews
13:15, KJV).

If you love money, you'll find it
brings all kinds of problems. "But
they that will be rich fall into tempta-
tion and a snare, and into many foolish and hurtful lusts, which drown
men in destruction and perdition"
(1 Timothy 6:9, KJV). "They that will
be rich" refers to those who are
determined that, no matter what, they
will be rich. "Perdition" means "loss."
When a person loves money, he is use-
less to God. Those are strong words,
but so were Jesus' words: "You cannot
serve God and riches."

I've heard people say, "I'm going to
make a million so I can give it to the
Lord." Don't try to make a million for
the Lord. The Lord isn't poor; He
doesn't need your fortune. Don't hide
your desire to be rich in such a
"spiritual" guise. "Seek ye first the
kingdom of God, and his righteousness" (Matthew 6:33, KJV). Let Him
decide whether you should have a mil-

lion. Set your heart on glorifying God, and if He makes you rich, that's gravy.

"You can't serve God and money." For money, Achan brought defeat on Israel's army and death to himself and to his family. For money, Balaam sinned and tried to curse God's people. For money, Delilah betrayed Samson and caused the slaughter of thousands. For money, Ananias and Sapphira became the first hypocrites in the church and God executed them. For money, Judas sold Jesus. Not very good company for money lovers, is it?

What does loving money lead to? For one thing, it persuades people to forget God.

Solomon was the author of most of the book of Proverbs, but Chapter 30 was written by a man named Agur. Solomon was rich beyond belief, but he got trapped in his riches and wanted more and more. He kept marrying foreign wives, to bring in more treasure and more treasure and more treasure. Thus, he brought Israel into idolatry and fouled up his own life.

As Agur saw what happened to Solomon, he prayed (Proverbs 30:8, NASB). "Give me neither poverty nor riches; feed me with the food that is my portion." Why? "Lest I be full and deny Thee and say, 'Who is the Lord?'

Or lest I be in want and steal, and profane the name of my God." Agur was saying, "Don't give me too much or I may worship my wealth instead of You. I'll become self-sufficient." But also, "Don't give me too little, or I'll steal to meet my needs." Love of money can make us forget God.

One of the most dangerous things about the love of money is that we begin to trust in it. We say, "Hey, everything is great in my life. I've got my bank account built up. I can take care of myself. I've got money for a rainy day." Are you trusting in your God or your gold? "If I have put my confidence in gold . . . If I have gloated because my wealth was great . . . I would have denied God above" (Job 31:24-28, NASB). "He who trusts in his riches will fall" (Proverbs 11:28, NASB). *The Living Bible* translates this, "Trust in your money and down you go!" The rest of the verse says, "Trust in God and flourish as a tree."

"Charge them that are rich in this world, that they be not high-minded, nor trust in uncertain riches, but in the living God" (1 Timothy 6:17, KJV). The rich should not flaunt their riches, but should rather acknowledge that their riches are from the living God. They should choose to "be rich in good works, ready to distribute, willing to communicate [share]" (vs. 18). Sadly, the more money people have, the less they're willing to part with it. Riches seem to obscure one's vision of eternal values.

When you love money, Satan can deceive you. In the parable of the sower in Mark 4, we read about the seed (the Word) being sown among thorns: "The cares of this world, and the deceitfulness of riches, and the lusts of other things entering in, choke the word" (vs. 19, KJV). When you have money, you can easily think you have everything. It lulls you into a false sense of complacency.

Love of money can lead a person to a place where he actually compromises biblical instruction. What would you sell out for? It has been said that every man has his price. What's yours? Someone has said that when money speaks, truth is silent. Is it in your life?

Some people (even Christians) would lie to get a job promotion. Some mute the testimony of Jesus so they won't be unpopular. That's selling out. Whatever your price, you can be sure Satan will come up with it. Some people would sell out for intellectualism, some for the body beautiful, some for golf, hunting, a new car. What's your price?

There was once a fancy banquet in a high-class New York hotel. A famous author sat next to a very beautiful and gracious woman. He was awestruck by her beauty. As they sat through the meal and talked, he finally asked her if she would spend the night with him for $100,000. She blushed, looked down, and finally said yes. He said, "Would you for ten dollars?" She protested, "What do you think I am?" He replied, "We've already established that; now we're working on the price." Do you get the message? It isn't the price that's the issue. It's what you are.

I hope you don't compromise biblical principles. I hope you can't be bought. I hope you are priceless. "Seek ye first the kingdom of God . . . these things shall be added unto you." When you start seeking something other than the kingdom of God and His righteousness, you've sold out.

Loving money can also lead you to build on an unstable foundation. Trusting money is like building a skyscraper on sinking sand. "Do not weary yourself to gain wealth, cease from your consideration of it. When you set your eyes on it, it is gone. For wealth certainly makes itself wings, like an eagle that flies toward the heavens" (Proverbs 23:4, 5, NASB).

Love of money can make you proud

and self-sufficient. "Beware lest you forget the Lord your God by not keeping His commandments and His ordinances and His statutes which I am commanding you today; lest, when you have eaten and are satisfied, and have built good houses and lived in them, and when your herds and your flocks multiply, and your silver and gold multiply, and all that you have multiplies, then your heart becomes proud, and you forget the Lord your God" (Deuteronomy 8:11-14, NASB). "The rich man is wise in his own conceit" (Proverbs 28:11, KJV).

"Why has the way of the wicked prospered? Why are all those who deal in treachery at ease? Thou hast planted them, they have also taken root; they grow, they have even produced fruit. Thou art near to their lips but far from their mind" (Jeremiah 12:1, 2, NASB). Overemphasis on money can do that to any one of us. With our mouths we can thank God for His blessings, yet leave no room for Him in our minds. This is hypocrisy.

If you consider money your own when it really is God's, you are actually stealing from God. "Will a man rob God? Yet ye have robbed me. But ye say, Wherein have we robbed thee? In tithes and offerings. . . . Bring ye all the tithes into the storehouse . . .

and I will pour you out a blessing" (Malachi 3:8, 10, KJV). You say, "I'd never do that. How would I ever get into God's storehouse?" Look in your pocket. That's God's storehouse, if you're a Christian. When you love money, you rob God.

Not only that, you rob others too. "Whoso hath this world's goods, and seeth his brother have need, and shutteth up his bowels of compassion from him, how dwelleth the love of God in him?" (1 John 3:17, KJV). You rob your brother if you use your (actually God's) money selfishly.

Earning money God's way. What does the Bible say about how you are to earn or obtain money? Quite a bit, and you dare not ignore it.

First of all, you are not to steal money. You say, "I would never do that." Really? "The wicked borrows and does not pay back" (Psalm 37:21, NASB). There are lots of ways to steal. Amos 8:5 and Hosea 12:7 talk about dishonest business tactics and cheating people out of their money. Perhaps contemporary prophets could point to eight hours' wages for five hours' work, or exaggerated deductions on an income tax return, or padded expense accounts, or extravagant credit card purchases. Stealing money is incompatible with the Christian life.

You are also not to exploit others by usury (high interest) or to overcharge them. If your brother has a need and you can help, give him what he needs. Don't try to make money off his trials.

You must also beware of defrauding people. James 5:4 pictures the money being withheld from laborers as crying out against the unjust employer. And those cries are heard by the Lord of hosts.

Gambling is apparently not an option for the Christian. An appeal to chance would seem to be incompatible with trust in the sovereignty of God.

We've talked about how you're *not* to get money. How are you to get it?

For one thing, you sometimes receive gifts. Whether it's a birthday present, or a love offering in response to some ministry you've had, this is a legitimate way of receiving cash. In Old Testament times, the firstborn son received the inheritance of all his father possessed. If your great-aunt dies and leaves you $50,000, take it as a gift from God.

The Christian can also make wise investments. Even one of Jesus' parable characters saw the value of letting money earn money (Matthew 25:27). I don't believe that God wants you to run the risk of wildcat investments and high-risk gambling speculations with His funds, but you can put them into wise investments.

Of course, the primary way to receive money (though not necessarily the most popular) is to work for it. "Six days shalt thou labor, and do all thy work" (Exodus 20:9, KJV). What about the four-day work week? I don't know; the Bible says "six." (Of course, we also "labor" on our homes, etc.) At any rate, "Let him who steals steal no longer, but rather let him labor" (Ephesians 4:28, NASB).

Six days of work, one day of rest. That was the Genesis formula. In other words, crowd your labor into six days. Really, you have enough for seven if you're working hard. Most (though not all) people in financial need don't know how to work. Many people who are chronically out of money are also chronically indolent. Obviously there are often extenuating circumstances in individual cases. But basically people who don't have anything don't work for anything.

Work is a divine principle, though not one we're especially excited about. "He who tills his land will have plenty of food, but he who follows empty pursuits will have poverty in plenty" (Proverbs 28:19, NASB). "In all labor there is profit, but mere talk leads only to poverty" (Proverbs 14:23, NASB). Work, you make money.

Talk, you don't. God doesn't put much of a premium on laziness.

God designed labor for our gain. The message of 2 Thessalonians 3:10 is certainly relevant to our age: "For even when we were with you, this we commanded you, that if any would not work, neither should he eat" (KJV). This verse isn't referring to those who genuinely can't find work, but it does say something about those who "can't" find a job because they don't want to. A man needs work for his own self-respect. "There are some which walk among you disorderly, working not at all, but are busybodies" (v. 11).

The Old Testament gives a great illustration of hard work: "Go to the ant, O sluggard, observe her ways and be wise, which having no chief officer or ruler prepares her food in the summer, and gathers her provision in the harvest" (Proverbs 6:6-8, NASB). The ant, on its own, without anyone making it work, stores away food for the winter. Yet we intelligent humans often need a fire built under us before we move. "The sluggard will not plow by reason of the cold; therefore shall he beg in harvest, and have nothing" (Proverbs 20:4, KJV). "If any provide not for his own, and specially for those of his own house, he hath denied the faith, and is worse than an infidel" (1 Timothy 5:8, KJV).

Another legitimate means of making money involves what is for many a forgotten art — saving. "There is precious treasure and oil in the dwelling of the wise, but a foolish man swallows it up" (Proverbs 21:20, NASB). A wise man sets aside some of his treasure and some of his oil for the unexpected. The fool uses it all up. *The Living Bible* translates this: "The wise man saves for the future, but the foolish man spends whatever he gets."

Getting back to the ants, "The ants are a people not strong, yet they prepare their meat in the summer" (Proverbs 30:25, KJV). This is saving! Ants are one of four creatures in the world that God exalts as being wise: ants, badgers, locusts, and spiders (see Proverbs 30:25-28). The ants don't make a great contribution to the world, but God extols them for a very interesting virtue: they prepare for the future. They're tiny animals that are easily stepped on, but they are smart enough to know they should stash food away for the time they're going to need it.

Future planning is not only reasonable, it's biblical. Maybe your future planning takes the form of long-term solid investments, or perhaps life insurance which allows you to set aside a certain amount of money to provide security for the future.

Being able to plan and to save requires financial self-control. One thing God has taught me in this regard is to always operate on a margin. If you don't, then you are presuming on the grace of God, and on His patience, hoping He'll overlook your irresponsibility and meet your need. You know how it goes. Instead of buying a practical, economical car, you buy a gas-guzzling ego-builder. And an extra TV, and this little luxury, that extra convenience, and . . . "Well, God will provide," you say as the bills surpass your checkbook balance.

Beware of extending yourself so far that you have to presume on God to rescue you from your own foolishness. David's prayer, "Keep back thy servant also from presumptuous sins," is appropriate for you (and me). When Satan took Jesus to the pinnacle of the Temple and said, "Cast yourself down so God will have to save you," Jesus answered, "It is written, Thou shalt not tempt the Lord thy God." Don't put yourself into a foolish situation and then demand that God extricate you. Leave a financial cushion for those unforeseen money needs.

Let's construct a hypothetical case

of a married couple who failed to apply biblical principles of financial planning.

This couple followed the great American way (buying things you don't need with money you don't have from people you don't even like). They soon had more obligations than income. Along the way they began to regularly support their local church and a few friends who had gone to the mission field. Before long they found they couldn't keep sending money to the missionaries and couldn't give what they should to the local church. They faced the possibility that they would even regress all the way to bankruptcy, loss of the car, loss of the house, loss of the job, and the loss of their testimony. Now they are limited as to what they can do for God, because they are having to pay for their foolishness with every dime they get. If God ever called them away to some mission field, they couldn't go.

God wants every Christian to have money — in fact, more than is needed. But He wants you to spend and save wisely. Some believers plan their budget on a sort of panmillennialism ("I don't know what the future holds, but it will all pan out"). God wants us to be a little more specific than that. This may mean having a budget. It certainly means having a priority list, planning, keeping records so you will know where you are. Remember, the money you are handling is God's money.

"Know well the condition of your flocks, and pay attention to your herds; for riches are not forever" (Proverbs 27:23, 24, NASB). You ought to know how many flocks you have; you ought to know what condition they are in; you ought to glorify God with good business sense. "Any enterprise is built by wise planning, becomes strong through common sense, and profits wonderfully by keeping abreast of the facts" (Proverbs 24:3, 4, TLB). "Owe no man anything, but to love one another" (Romans 13:8, KJV). The only debt you ought to have is love, and you can't ever unload that one. Just keep paying, paying, paying love.

Do you know what happens when you owe somebody something? Now I'm not talking about faithfully making your house payment every month. I'm talking about when you overextend yourself, when you owe money and can't pay it. "The borrower is servant to the lender" (Proverbs 22:7, KJV). You are a slave to your creditors. And this is a direct violation of biblical principles. "You are bought with a price; be not ye the servants [or slaves] of men" (1 Corinthians 7:23, KJV). A Christian should always be free enough to respond to whatever God wants him to do at any time, without being held back by financial chains. You need to have a pilgrim mentality as you walk in this world.

God warns you to not become a loan company. If some guy is bugging you to death, the easiest way to get rid of him is to loan him money. You'll probably never see him again. In some cases you may figure it's worth the investment. Is it?

You say, "What if a person comes to me and says he needs some money to buy something he doesn't really need?" If it isn't a necessity, don't loan it to him. If it is a necessity, still don't loan it to him — give it to him. If we see a brother in need and refuse to let ourselves care, we are shutting off the love of God (check out 1 John 3:17).

Also remember that "it is poor judgment to countersign another's note, to become responsible for his debts" (Proverbs 17:18, TLB). The Bible is really practical.

So the Scripture says that there are three principles by which God wants us to acquire money: work, save, and plan carefully. I find it exciting to realize that God really does want you

to have a certain amount of money —
not just enough for the bare necessities, but a little extra so when the
Spirit says, "There's a need over
there," you can help. Because you
have this margin, you can supply that
need.

Using and misusing money. You say,
"John, I'm glad God wants me to have
money, but evidently he doesn't really
understand my situation, because I
never have enough." When you're
short on dough, take this little test: (1)
Do I need (not want) more money? Is
it really a need? (2) Is God testing my
faith? (3) Have I misused what He has
already given me? (4) Have I violated
biblical principles?

If God gives you enough money for
all your needs (and He does!) and you
still don't have enough (you think),
then maybe you missed some of God's
instructions. The Bible gives the fol-
lowing reasons for not having
enough:

Stinginess. One of the reasons you
don't have enough is because you
didn't give enough away. Proverbs
11:24 says, "There is one who scatters,
yet increases all the more, and there is
one who withholds what is justly due,
but it results only in want" (NASB).
This means that maybe you have been

too stingy with your money. In your selfishness, you have failed to put yourself in the place where God will multiply your resources.

Hastiness. Proverbs 21:5 says, "Everyone who is hasty comes surely to poverty" (NASB). I am learning never to buy anything the day that I decide I want it, because invariably my action will prove to have been hasty. So I'll talk it over with my wife and sleep on it and wait a week. If it's a whim, the desire will go away. But I have to watch for hastiness.

Stubbornness. This is another thing that can cause you trouble. Proverbs 13:18 says, "Poverty and shame will come to him who neglects discipline" (NASB). If you are an undisciplined person, you are going to have trouble with money. One of the areas that we all need to improve in is discipline, particularly with regard to finances.

Laziness. Maybe you don't have any money because you are lazy. "Do not love sleep, lest you become poor; open your eyes, and you will be satisfied with food" (Proverbs 20:13, NASB). "Drowsiness will clothe a man with rags" (Proverbs 23:21, NASB). The first part of that verse warns us about another enemy . . .

Indulgence. "The heavy drinker and the glutton will come to poverty." A lot of people eat up their money. One reason not to be overweight is just that. It is a waste of money. Picture yourself stuffing dollar bills into your mouth, instead of food!

Craftiness. Do you know why many people don't have money? Proverbs 28:19 says, "He who tills his land will have plenty of food, but he who follows empty pursuits will have poverty in plenty" (NASB). Some people make unwise investments, putting their money in things that don't work. I heard a man say recently that most con men (because they are sharp and intelligent) would make ten times more by being honest than they make by being dishonest.

If you have to say that you do not have enough money, maybe it is because you are a little stingy, a little hasty, a little stubborn, a little lazy, a little indulgent, or a little crafty. Those are character traits you ought to eliminate from your life. God wants you to have money, and He wants you to enjoy what you have. He also wants you to make it available for His use.

So, it's not wrong to have money, but how you use it is the real test. And the Bible tells us how we are to spend our money.

For one thing, you are to provide for the needs of your family. "If any provide not for his own, and specially for those of his own house, he hath denied the faith, and is worse than an infidel" (1 Timothy 5:8, KJV). That's serious talk, showing the importance God places on your taking care of your family.

God also wants you to use your money to pay your debts, promptly. God (through Elisha) told a woman to "go, sell the oil and pay your debt, and you and your sons can live on the rest" (2 Kings 4:7, NASB). In other words, if you can't pay your debts, sell something you have, pay your debts, and live on what's left.

You can use your money to help others, too. I am again reminded of 1 John 3:17 (we've already seen this verse a few times, but its importance warrants another look at it): "But whoever has the world's goods, and beholds his brother in need and closes his heart against him, how does the love of God abide in him?" (NASB). The phrase "closes his heart" can be literally translated "shuts up his bowels," "bowels" being the Hebrew expression for "seat of compassion; emotion; gut-level feeling." If you see somebody in need, and it doesn't hit you in the gut so you can't help but give to him, then you don't have God's love for him. God wants each of us to be a Good Samaritan. And who is your neighbor? Anyone who is in your path and has a need. Anyone.

Acts 2:45 tells us that the early Christians "sold their possessions and goods, and parted them to all men, as every man had need" (KJV). As I said earlier, some take this to be a sort of Christian communism, but that's because they don't really understand the Greek tense. The verbs "sold" and "parted" are both in the imperfect tense, which denotes continuous action. The verse should read, "And they were selling their possessions and goods and were parting them to all men as every man had need." It does not say that all at once they sold and all at once they parted. It simply says that all the believers were selling their goods and giving the money to those who had need as needs arose. This was giving and self-sacrifice for the need of another, not a pooling of everything in a kind of communism.

The Bible nowhere advocates that all monies be put into a common pot and doled out by some hierarchy. The same thing appears in Acts 4:34: "Neither was there any among them that lacked: for as many as were possessors of lands or houses were selling them, and were bringing the prices of the things that were sold, and laid them down at the apostles' feet: and distribution was made unto every man according as he had need" (KJV). When a person had a need, another was willing to sell something and use the money to meet that man's need.

All of us who know Jesus Christ are God's stewards and are entrusted with His money. "Moreover, it is required of stewards that one be found trustworthy" (1 Corinthians 4:2, NASB). During your lifetime God entrusts you with an incredible amount of money. If you start earning about $15,000 a year when you are twenty and earn it until you are sixty, you will earn well over half a million dollars. Will you be able to say that your half-million was used purposefully? Oh, not all directly for the Lord, but purposefully. (After all, if you are a Christian, living in the will of God, even paying your electric bill is "giving" to the work of the Lord. You are part of that work. God not only works in churches and religious organizations or programs; he is at work in His people.)

You may think I'm making a theological mountain out of a mundane molehill, but I believe (on the authority of Jesus, no less) that proper handling of your finances is a key to spiritual fruit in your life. Jesus said, "He that is faithful in that which is least is faithful also in much: and he that is unjust in the least is unjust also in much. If therefore ye have not been faithful in the unrighteous mammon, who will commit to your trust the true riches?" (Luke 16:10, 11, KJV).

Some people say, "I don't know why I don't have a ministry for the Lord. I can't understand why I don't see much fruit in my life." If you aren't faithful with money, do you think God can use you with souls? I know of many men who are out of the pastorate and out of the ministry today for the simple reason that they couldn't handle money, and God would never commit souls to them. This is serious business. God help us to be faithful stewards.

All of this becomes a barometer of your Christian life. How you handle money is just like everything else — how you treat your wife or husband, how you train your children, how you work at your job, how you act in your relationship with other believers, how you maintain your prayer life and Bible study habits — all this is an indicator of your spiritual life. Money is no different from the rest. The credibility of your Christianity is manifest in the handling of your funds.

Every dime that God gives you becomes a test of your loyalty to him. Every penny you have can be used to glorify God. All the money you have (I deliberately did not say "your money," because it's not yours) can honor God. Remember, you cannot serve God and money. Perhaps you think a tenth of your cash is the Lord's, and the rest is yours to use however you want. No! One hundred percent of every dime you get should be used to glorify God. This doesn't mean that you should give it all to missionaries or to your church. It just means that you must use it as your Lord directs you, for His glory.

CHAPTER THREE
"Will a Man Rob God?"

THE MAJOR money issue in Scripture is not how you feel about it, or even how you spend it. The primary concern of Scripture is how you *give* it. All that I've said so far is just an introduction to this strategic subject — giving money God has entrusted to you.

This subject gets a little painful. I squirm myself sometimes when I think about my responsibility (and irresponsibility) in this area. But it dominates Scripture and thus must be too important a subject for us to by-pass.

The Apostle Paul commended the Macedonian Christians not only for their generous giving but because they "first gave their own selves to the Lord" (2 Corinthians 8:5, KJV). That's where it all begins. Give yourself to the Lord first, or else the rest is somewhat meaningless.

Of course, the Lord does want you to give to your brother and sister in need. He wants you to give to the work of Jesus Christ and to invest your dollars for God. But giving is not God's way of raising money. Giving is God's way of raising children. Every time you give sacrificially, you give a little of your selfishness away. And when you give, others are blessed and God is glorified. (See 2 Corinthians 9 for the rundown on this.)

We'll look at Old Testament giving in this chapter and New Testament giving in the next. But before diving into the Old Testament, I want to say this: the underlying pattern of giving has been the same in all periods of history. God has made some surface changes, but underneath His instructions now are the same as they were in the time of Moses and even before. There is no difference.

As we examine giving in Old Testament times, we will take a good, long look at tithing. Are we to tithe today? Does God want our 10 percent today?

Those who believe we should tithe today reason thus:

Abraham and Jacob tithed before the Mosaic law was instituted. In other words, tithing existed before the law. And since there was tithing before the law, there should also be tithing after the law, because it is a universal principle. There was tithing before the Mosaic law, during the law, and it should follow after. It is a continuous responsibility.

There is a problem in saying that anything before the law was also a norm after the law. The sabbath was before the law. So should we quit meeting on Sunday? The sacrificial system was initiated in the Garden. So should we be offering lambs today? I don't think so (and Galatians, Hebrews, and other Scriptures support this).

God's plan for giving – before Moses. Giving before Moses (like giving in all periods of history) fell into two categories: required giving, and freewill giving. These two kinds of giving are side by side throughout the Scriptures.

Freewill giving. The word "tithe" does appear in Genesis, in connection with Abraham and with Jacob.

The Hebrew word translated "tithe" is *ma aser*, which simply means "a tenth part." The Greek counterpart to this was *dekate*, "the tenth." This wasn't a religious word, but a mathematical one. It could be used in theology or mathematics. It had only to do with a percentage.

The important thing to see here is that in Genesis the word "tithe" did not refer to a required offering, but a voluntary one. The tithes of Abraham and Jacob were freewill gifts and were not, strictly speaking, the same as tithes given under Mosaic law.

The concept of a tithe was not limited to the Bible. We know from ancient sources that man has always used ten as the basic number for counting systems. This was apparently because he had ten fingers and ten toes, and used this as the foundation for his figuring. Throughout man's history he has used ten as a basis of measurement, as well as a symbol of completion.

Many pagan deities were honored by the giving of a tenth. The reason? The number ten represented totality or completeness. Thus the giving of a tenth symbolized the giving of the whole. To give your god a tenth represented giving your all, total surrender.

So ten was a common number in presenting offerings to the gods, even well before Abraham. The idea of a tithe was not new in the days of the Hebrew patriarchs.

God did not institute tithing in Genesis — neither in Genesis 4 (Cain and Abel), Genesis 8 (Noah), Genesis 12 and 14 (Abraham), nor in Genesis 28 (Jacob). In each case there was no statement from God regarding tithing. There is no universal law of tithing stated anywhere in Scripture. Let's look at this in more detail.

In Genesis 4 we find the first offering to God in Scripture, that of Cain and Abel. The interesting thing about this was that it was essentially a voluntary offering, a free choice on the part of the two brothers. It simply says in verse 3 that in the process of time Cain offered the fruit of the ground and Abel brought the firstlings of the flock.

As far as we can tell from Scripture itself, God had not specifically asked them to do this. They did it voluntarily. There had been no universal law as to how much; God didn't say, "I want one of those, or four of these." But there was apparently some revelation about what was to be offered. Cain was disobedient to the information they had been given about this (the sacrifice was to be an animal sacrifice, so there would be blood shed, an early preview of Christ's death for us).

But there was no requirement of percentage, or quantity, or frequency, or that sort of thing. Nor did God say the offering must be made on a certain day at a certain time at a certain place. This was a voluntary offering. They acted on their own initiative.

And as far as we know, this first offering was in no way related to the tenth. It's doubtful that Abel had only ten sheep, for example.

Let's move on to Chapter 8, the story of Noah. When the flood subsided, Noah immediately went out to build an altar and make an offering to God. Verse 20 says he presented burnt offerings of every clean beast and every clean fowl. This was a completely voluntary offering. God had not commanded Noah to do this (so obviously no percentage had been stipulated). The offering was a spontaneous expression of Noah's gratitude. We have no reason to assume a tenth was involved in any way.

In Chapter 12 Abram was given the wonderful call of God to be the leader of a nation. In response to that (verse

7) he built an altar to the Lord. This offering to the Lord had no command, no stipulation, no requirement. Abram freely responded to the wonderful promise of God and said thank-you to God by way of an offering. In 13:18 he built another altar to the Lord, this time in Hebron. This was voluntary, not a response to a special command of God. This was freewill giving involving no stipulated amount, no requirements, no stated figures, no percentages, no frequency, as revealed in Genesis 12 or 13.

The first actual mention of the tithe is found in Genesis 14:18-20: "And Melchizedek king of Salem brought forth bread and wine: and he was the priest of the most high God. And he blessed him, and said, Blessed be Abram of the most high God, possessor of heaven and earth: And blessed be the most high God, which hath delivered thine enemies into thy hand. And he gave him tithes of all" (KJV).

Abram had just returned from fighting Chedorlaomer and other kings in the valley of Shaveh. He had been victorious and had taken a tremendous amount of spoil and treasure. On his way back home he ran into the king of Salem (the ancient name of Jerusalem). This king's name was Melchizedek, who according to the book of Hebrews was both priest and king. He was the priest of the most high God, verse 18 tells us.

When Abram saw God's representative, he naturally wanted to express thanks to God for the victory. So what did he do? "He gave him tithes of all" (v. 20). Did God tell him to give a tenth? No. It was spontaneous. Abram was never told to give a tenth. In fact, this is the only recorded time he ever gave a tithe during his 160 years on earth.

By the way, verse 20 doesn't necessarily mean that Abram gave a tenth of everything he owned. He gave a tenth of something he had taken in the battle. It wasn't a tenth of his total income or wealth, nor was it an annual tithe. Hebrews 7:4 tells us that he gave Melchizedek a "tenth of the spoils," but the Greek word used here for "spoils" is *akrothinion*, which is literally "the pinnacle, the top, the top of the heap." Abram gave a tithe of the top of the heap. This could mean that he didn't give a tenth of all the spoils, but he gave a tenth of the best of the spoils. Considering that he had taken treasure from five kings, it may well be that a tenth of all the spoils would be more than one priest could accept or handle.

But the important thing to see here

is that this tithe was a one-time thing.
There is no record that Abraham ever
did this again. And it was free, voluntary, totally motivated by his heart,
not by divine command. He chose to
give. And he gave what was common
to give, a tenth, representative of his
giving all that he had. To Abraham
and to his contemporaries, ten meant
completeness.

Now let's go to the other mention of
a tithe in the book of Genesis. "Then
Jacob made a vow, saying, 'If God will
be with me and will keep me on this
journey that I take, and will give me
food to eat and garments to wear, and
I return to my father's house in safety,
then the Lord will be my God. And
this stone, which I have set up as a pil-
lar, will be God's house; and of all that
Thou dost give me I will surely give a
tenth to Thee' " (Genesis 28:20-22,
NASB).

Do you realize what Jacob was really
trying to do? He was trying to bribe
God. "Hey, God, give me a safe trip
and bread and clothes, and I'll let you
be my God. I'll even build an altar and
give You a tenth of everything I
have." He was attempting to buy
God's blessings. Jacob was obviously at
a low point spiritually. His motive for
the tithe was far from sincere.

You can read this passage a dozen

times and you will not find any mention of God's commanding Jacob to give Him a tithe. The offering was completely voluntary. There was no obligation, and in fact, as we have seen, in this case the tithe was displeasing to God because of the reason Jacob gave it. Our games and pretenses don't set well with the Lord.

So we see many offerings in Genesis, two of them tithes. But they were all voluntary. Abraham and Jacob were not conforming to divine fiat, but were merely giving a tenth as a symbol of giving all. There is no case for tithing as a pre-Mosaic requirement of God. Would God require something without telling men what He required? Yet Genesis gives no record of God's demanding a tenth.

Required giving. A tithe was not required, but there was required giving before the Mosaic law. Sound like doubletalk? Genesis 41 describes a required giving of money or of possessions. (During most of the time recorded in Genesis, people didn't give money at all because their exchange wasn't money; they gave animals or seed or land.)

The chapter I mentioned tells how Joseph, who had been sold into slavery in Egypt by his brothers, interpreted a dream Pharaoh couldn't

58

handle. There will be seven years of fruitful crops and seven years of famine, said Joseph, so we had better prepare for the famine. How? "Let Pharaoh take action to appoint overseers in charge of the land, and let him exact a fifth of the produce of the land of Egypt in the seven years of abundance" (Genesis 41:34, NASB). For seven years, collect a tax of 20 percent of the crops. Here was the first IRS and the first federal income tax. And like it or not, it was introduced by God. This taxation was to support the nation of Egypt. The 20 percent collected throughout the fat years would supply the people with enough food for the lean years.

We see this again in Genesis 47:24 — "And at the harvest you shall give a fifth to Pharaoh, and four-fifths shall be your own for seed of the field and for your food and for those of your households and as food for your little ones" (NASB). God was saying, "Four parts are for you — some to plant in the field, some to eat, some for the needs of your household, and some for your kids; the fifth part goes to the government." Again it is clear that the 20 percent was given for the funding of the national government.

Freewill giving was directed toward the Lord and was offered personally, as a response of love and sacrifice.

Required giving was directed toward the national government, for the supply of the needs of the people. This has continued on, right through the present day.

Required giving – From Moses to Jesus.
Let's move on to the time of Moses. What about tithing then? Most Christians think that Israel's tithing involved giving a tenth. They are mistaken, as we will see.

Leviticus 27:30 mentions a tithe called "the Lord's" tithe (sometimes called the Levites' tithe because according to Numbers 18 this tithe was divided among the Levites). "And all the tithe of the land, whether of the seed of the land, or of the fruit of the tree, is the Lord's: it is holy unto the Lord" (KJV).

Of course, the Levites, one of the twelve tribes of Israel, were the priests and Temple assistants. The taxation of the rest of the tribes went to supply the needs of the Levites. Thus this was a Levite tithe.

God was saying, "Ten percent of all of your land and seeds and fruit is Mine." If a man wanted to keep his fruit, "he shall add thereto the fifth part thereof" (vs. 31). In other words, he could give an extra portion and use money instead of fruit. But concerning the tithe of the herd of the flock, "whatsoever passeth under the rod, the tenth shall be holy unto the Lord. He shall not search whether it be good or bad, neither shall he change it . . . it shall not be redeemed" (vv. 32, 33). In other words, you could give money in exchange for the land and the seed and the fruit, but you could not redeem the animals. Those you had to give.

So the first tithe was 10 percent of the people's produce and animals. The emphasis here is on quantity. The tithe already belonged to God. This was not a freewill offering. It was His already, and those who didn't give it would be robbing God. "Will a man rob God? Yet ye have robbed me. But ye say, Wherein have we robbed thee? In tithes and offerings" (Malachi 3:8, KJV).

This tithe was given to the tribe of priests to support them. Because their religious responsibilities were a full-time ministry, they didn't have the opportunity to earn their own living. They were, in a sense, the government of their land. Israel wasn't a democracy, but a theocracy. Who was the ruler of Israel? God. Who were His vice-regents? The priests. So when you come right down to it, the Levites' tithe paid the salaries of those who ran the country. In other words, this tithe was actually a form of taxation. It was required giving.

So the Israelites did give 10 percent, to begin with. But Deuteronomy 12 mentions a second tithe. "When you cross the Jordan and live in the land which the Lord your God is giving you to inherit, and He gives you rest from all your enemies around you so that you live in security, then it shall come about that the place in which the Lord your God shall choose for His name to dwell, there you shall bring all that I command you: your burnt offerings and your sacrifices, your tithes and the contribution of your hand, and all your choice votive offerings which you will vow to the Lord . . . You are not allowed to eat within your gates the tithe of your grain, or new wine, or oil, or the first-born of your herd or flock, or any of your votive offerings which you vow, or your freewill offerings, or the contribution of your hand. But you shall eat them before the Lord your God in the place which the Lord your God will choose, you and your son and daughter, and your male and female servants, and the Levite who is within your gates; and you shall re-joice before the Lord your God in all your undertakings" (vv. 10, 11, 17, 18, NASB).

This is another tithe, another 10 percent. This 10 percent was to be taken to Jerusalem and was to be eaten by family, friends, servants, and the priests in the sanctuary. This tithe would stimulate devotion to the Lord and promote unity in the family. It was kind of like national potluck. It made everybody share.

This tithe, called the festival tithe, perpetuated the religious and social life of the nation. So the Levites' tithe supported the government people. This one helped the religious, social, and cultural community by increasing love for God and by teaching individuals to share with others. It taught community and social involvement.

We're already up to 20 percent (or more if you redeemed some goods), but we're not through yet. Deuteronomy 14:28 mentions a third tithe: "At the end of three years thou shalt bring forth all the tithe of thine increase the same year, and shalt lay it up within thy gates" (KJV). This tithe was for "the Levite, . . . the stranger, and the fatherless, and the widow" (v. 29), and so was called the poor tithe. This was a welfare program for the poor, the widows, the people who didn't have anything to eat.

This brings the Israelites' "tithe" up to 23+ percent. Those who say the Jew gave 10 percent have a partial picture. The Jew gave 23+ percent in these three tithes. If you teach tithing, do you know what you teach? You teach 23+ percent a year giving. That's right. Study it for yourself. That's exactly what the Old Testament tithing amounted to.

The three tithes funded the Levites (government), a national feast (community), and help for the poor (welfare). This is all funding for the national entity. All three of these were taxation, not freewill giving to God. Tithing was never giving to God. It was always taxation.

And the Jew wasn't done yet. Leviticus 19:9, 10 describes Israel's profit-sharing plan: "And when ye reap the harvest of your land, thou shalt not wholly reap the corners of thy field, neither shalt thou gather the gleanings of thy harvest. And thou shalt not glean thy vineyard, neither shalt thou gather every grape of the vineyard; thou shalt leave them for the poor and stranger: I am the Lord your God" (KJV). They were in effect giving part of their produce to the poor.

And there's still more! Nehemiah 10:32, 33 tells about a third of a shekel Temple tax they had to pay to buy materials for Temple offerings. Exodus 23:10, 11 demanded a sabbath rest for the land every seventh year. In other words, they forfeited an entire year's earnings off the land to let the land rest. During that same sabbath year, the Israelites had to set all debts aside as paid. Ten percent is a far cry from what it cost them to exist within the theocracy of Israel. I would say that, conservatively, a Jew paid a minimum of 25 percent a year required giving. But this was not freewill giving to the Lord. This was taxation, required giving.

Freewill giving — from Moses to Jesus. In addition to all this, there was voluntary giving in Old Testament Israel. This included firstfruits giving and freewill offerings. The emphasis here was not on quantity or a percentage, but on the attitude of the giver and the quality of his gift.

If you ask, "But how much were they supposed to give?" you're missing the point. It wasn't supposed to be any particular amount. You mean they could give whatever they wanted to? I'm supposed to tell my congregation that? The Board will never buy it! (Do you serve a Board or the Lord?)

Let's take a closer look at Israel's freewill giving. It did make sense and it did work!

If you want an interesting study, do a rundown on the firstfruit offerings. "All the best of the oil, all the best of the wine, and of the wheat, the first-fruits of them which they shall offer unto the Lord, them have I given thee" (Numbers 18:12, KJV).

The Israelite gave the firstfruits of his crop to God. When the firstfruits came up, he would scoop them up and take them to the Temple to offer to the Lord. The beauty of this was that he hadn't yet harvested the crop, and he didn't even know how much he would have. He was giving away the firstfruits without knowing what the rest of the crop would be like. He was investing with God, voluntarily. He was living by faith. No specific amount was required in this.

He was believing God, and God was saying, "If you will give Me the first-fruits, right off the top, before you even know how much you're going to have, if you'll trust Me that much, I'll bring in your full harvest." We see this magnificent promise in Proverbs 3:9, 10: "Honor the Lord with thy sub-stance, and with the firstfruits of all thine increase: So shall thy barn be filled with plenty, and thy presses shall burst out with new wine" (KJV). Honor God with every penny that you have and give Him the firstfruits, and He'll fill your barns and your presses will burst forth with new wine — that's God's promise to Israel.

Of course, God's promises to Israel were fulfilled temporally; we cannot make the exact same statement for New Testament promises, which are fulfilled spiritually. You say, "I knew it, I knew it. I'll give God all my money and all I'll get out of it is spiritual blessings." Which would you rather have, answered prayer or a bigger bank account; inner contentment or a new yacht? Spiritual blessings are always better. (But 2 Corinthians 9:10 reminds us that God won't let us starve either.)

So the Israelites were to give God the firstfruits, the best. God told the people (through Malachi) that He was displeased with their sacrificing the blind and the lame, the worst animals they had. They kept the best for themselves and so forfeited God's blessing. You shouldn't spend all your money on yourself and sock away money in some great fund to take care of yourself, then trickle a little bit to God. That isn't the firstfruits. It's when you give Him the cream of what you have and keep a little bit for yourself that He'll prosper and reward you.

Proverbs 11:24 (NASB) says, "There is one who scatters, yet increases all the more, and there is one who withholds what is justly due, but it results only in want." In other words, if you give liberally, you will receive even more; but if you selfishly hold on to what you have, you will be poor. "The generous man will be prosperous, and he who waters will himself be watered" (v. 25).

The firstfruits offering was an act of faith. That's the way God wanted His children to live. Since they loved Him and believed in Him and trusted Him, they were willing to do it. Give God whatever you want, give Him the best that you have, take it right off the top — and He'll fill your barn. Do you believe that? Do you really believe that you can skim off the best you've got and give it to God without coming out short? That's the way the Israelites gave. No amount, no percentage — just voluntary, sacrificial giving.

Not only was tithing not New Testament giving, it wasn't even Old Testament giving. It was taxation. Giving is by nature the freewill sharing of whatever your thankful heart desires to give, and the heart set on God gives the best that it has.

Some Christians tell me, "MacArthur, if we took all this seriously, it would mess up our church. People wouldn't tithe and we'd always be short on money." Well, if that's really true, your and/or your church's problem isn't with me but with the Scripture. What do the Scriptures say? That's the crucial question.

Let's move on to the second aspect of voluntary giving, the freewill offering. "And the Lord spake unto Moses, saying, Speak unto the children of Israel, that they bring me an offering: of every man that giveth it willingly with his heart ye shall take my offering" (Exodus 25:1, 2, KJV). Here was God's chance to specify what He wanted given to Him. All he had to say was, "Give Me a tenth." Instead, he said, "Give willingly, from the heart." This heart attitude was emphasized over and over again, as we will see. There were no big posters asking HAVE YOU GIVEN YOUR TENTH? They were just to do whatever their hearts said to do.

In case you want some evidence: "And Moses spake unto all the congregation of the children of Israel, saying, This is the thing which the Lord commanded, saying, Take ye from among you an offering unto the Lord: whosoever is of a willing heart, let him bring an offering of the Lord; gold, and silver, and brass, and purple, and scarlet, and fine linen, and goats' hair, and ram's skin dyed red, and badger's skins, and shittim wood, and oil for the light, and spices for anointing oil, and for the sweet incense, and onyx stones to be set for the ephod, and for the breastplate. And every wise-hearted among you shall come, and make all that the Lord hath commanded" (Exodus 35:4-10, KJV). In other words, just come and bring whatever is on your heart or whatever you have. I like that.

Look at verses 21, 22: "And they came, every one whose heart stirred him up, and every one whom his spirit made willing, and they brought the Lord's offering to the work of the tabernacle of the congregation, and for all his service, and for the holy garments. And they came, both men and women, as many as were willing-hearted." Do you get the idea? What is God really after in giving? A willing heart. "Thou shalt give unto the Lord thy God, according as the Lord thy God hath blessed thee . . . Every man shall give as he is able, according to the blessing of the Lord thy God which he hath given thee" (Deuteronomy 16:10, 17, KJV).

There's more: "And they spake unto Moses, saying, The people bring much more than enough for the service of the work, which the Lord commanded to make. And Moses gave commandment, saying, Let neither man nor woman make any more work for the offering of the sanctuary. So the people were restrained from bringing" (Exodus 36:5-7, KJV). Have you ever heard a church say, "Please don't give any more money"? This should happen in our churches. When people believe in a ministry, they should give "much more than enough." Giving that is done with true motivation will go beyond the immediate need. We're beginning to see the reality of that in our church as our people are beginning to operate on these principles. In some months we can't spend the money as fast as they give it.

Do you see what I'm saying? Required giving was taxation. Freewill giving came out of a willing heart. And when God's people believe in a specific ministry or project, their hearts are willing to give sacrificially.

For example, consider 1 Chronicles 29. David was thinking about getting everything together for the building of the glorious Temple that Solomon would erect, and "the people rejoiced, for that they offered willingly, because with perfect heart they offered willingly to the Lord: and David the king also rejoiced with great joy. Wherefore David blessed the Lord before all

71

the congregation" (vv. 9, 10, KJV). They had a praise session there, getting ready to collect the offering.

David prayed, "O Lord our God, all this store that we have prepared to build thee a house for thine holy name cometh of thine hand, and all is thine own" (v. 16). Much was given to build God's house. Do you know what kind of Temple that was? Absolutely unbelievable. Everything was overlaid in gold. We too should be free in the Spirit of God to give superabundantly. If we sow bountifully, we will reap bountifully.

Summary: Tithing, required to fund the theocracy, was equivalent to our modern-day tax structure. The three tithes took care of government salaries, the social and religious life of the nation, and a welfare system. Tithes were not freewill gifts. The tithes didn't belong to the people, so how could they give them away? The tithe was the Lord's. The Israelites didn't tithe a straight 10 percent, but nearly 25 percent. Tithes were not gifts at all, but were required giving.

On the other side of the coin, freewill giving was purely voluntary and personal. Motivated only by the thankfulness and love of the individual believer, it was to be proportionate as that individual decided before God. No amount or frequency of giving was ever stipulated. In fact, very little was said about freewill giving except that generosity and liberality will be rewarded by God Himself.

CHAPTER FOUR
"As God Hath Prospered Him"

WHAT DOES
the New Testament say about giving?
Basically it says the same thing the
Old Testament said: pay your taxes
(required giving); give God whatever
you want (freewill giving). New
Testament teaching on giving is more
clearly defined than that in the Old
Testament, but actually the pattern is
the same throughout the Bible. I
realize these statements do not agree
with the view of many Christians who
see Old Testament giving in one light

and New Testament giving in another. But again, what do the Scriptures really teach?

Required giving in the New Testament. Remember that in Old Testament times the tithes that were exacted from the Jews — the Temple tax, the land sabbath rest, the special profit-sharing tax (leaving the corners unharvested, for the poor) — all of this was taxation. At the time the Gospels were written, the Jews were still under these laws. So it was proper for a Jew to continue to pay his tithes, etc. The taxation system was still going. The Temple treasury still had thirteen trumpet-shaped receptacles in which the people put their tax money. In addition to that, the Romans were exacting exorbitant taxes from them. So the Jews were still obligated by Mosaic law, as well as by Roman law, to pay their taxes.

Jesus remarked about this repeatedly in the Gospels. For example: "And when they had come to Capernaum, those who collected the two-drachma tax came to Peter, and said, 'Does your teacher not pay the two-drachma tax?' He said, 'Yes.' And when he came into the house, Jesus spoke to him first, saying, 'What do you think, Simon? From whom do the kings of the earth collect customs or poll-tax, from their sons or from strangers?' And upon his saying, 'From strangers,' Jesus said to him, 'Consequently the sons are exempt. But, lest we give them offense, go to the sea, and throw in a hook, and take the first fish that comes up; and when you open its mouth, you will find a stater [shekel]. Take that and give it to them for you and Me' " (Matthew 17:24-27, NASB).

In 1 John 2:6 it says that we are to walk as Jesus walked. Jesus paid His taxes. We are to pay ours. I think it's exciting to see Matthew present this, because Matthew depicted Christ as King. Even though Christ was indeed King (in fact, King of kings), He still obeyed the law and paid His taxes.

Let's talk a little bit about Jesus' strangers/sons comments. Obviously kings don't tax their own sons. They work around that. They tax strangers. Jesus was saying that in a sense we shouldn't need to pay taxes; we're children of the King. But to avoid offending our society, we are to pay taxes.

On this occasion Peter got his tax money out of a fish. If that was still in vogue, about April 1 the beach would be lined with Christians from San Diego to Seattle. God is not still operating on that basis, unfortunately.

The point of the passage is simply

this: Jesus paid His taxes. He advocated what the Father advocated in the Old Testament — pay your taxes. This is required giving.

We see the same thing in Matthew 22:15-22: "Then the Pharisees went and counseled together how they might trap Him in what He said. [They spent a career doing that and losing]. And they sent their disciples to Him, along with the Herodians, saying, 'Teacher, we know that you are truthful and teach the way of God in truth, and defer to no one; for you are not partial to any. Tell us therefore, what do You think? Is it lawful to give a poll-tax to Caesar, or not?' " If Jesus said pay your Roman taxes, the Jews would be down on Him for being a pro-Roman traitor. If He said don't pay the tax, the Romans would be after Him for being an insurrectionist. The Jews were sure they had Him between a rock and a hard place.

"But Jesus perceived their malice, and said, 'Why are you testing Me, you hypocrites? Show me the coin used for the poll-tax.' And they brought Him a denarius. And He said to them, 'Whose likeness and inscription is this?' They said to Him, 'Caesar's.' Then He said to them, 'Then render to Caesar the things that are Caesar's; and to God the things that are God's.' "

What a tremendous answer! This money must go to Caesar, but give the important things to God, Jesus seemed to be saying. "And hearing this, they marveled, and leaving Him, they went away."

In Matthew 23:23 Jesus called the Pharisees "hypocrites" (for the fifth time in the same conversation, and he had three more to go). "Ye pay tithe of mint and anise and cummin [if they had ten seeds, they were giving one seed to the priest, etc.], and have omitted the weightier matters of the law, judgment, mercy, and faith" (KJV). Jesus didn't criticize these legalists for paying the tithe. Jesus acknowledged it was right for them to do that. That was their taxation system. But they ignored the things that really mattered; that's why they were called hypocrites.

The only other mention of tithing in the Gospels is found in Luke 18:12, where the hypocritical Pharisee boasted to God, "I fast twice in the week, I give tithes of all that I possess" (KJV). Actually, paying your taxes isn't anything to boast about — you're supposed to do that.

The remaining New Testament mention of tithing (Hebrews 7:1-4) had to do with Abraham giving Melchizedek a tenth, not because God told him to but because he wanted to.

This was not a directive for the New Testament church, but simply a recollection of an Old Testament event.

In the New Testament (as in the Old), required giving took the form of taxation to support a national government. The Jew was to pay the Temple tax to support what was still a theocratic government (though not perhaps as fully as in Old Testament days), and was also to pay Rome what was due Rome.

Furthermore, nowhere does the New Testament demand or even hint (and there are plenty of places where it easily could have) that the Christian is supposed to tithe. Tithing as such has no bearing on the church at all.

You say, "But we're not under the Jewish economy. The tithes (taxes) funded the national government of Israel, God's earthly people. America isn't a theocracy!" Granted, America isn't a theocracy (no doubt about that!), but that doesn't free you from paying taxes. All government is God-ordained.

"Let every soul be subject unto the higher powers. For there is no power but of God: the powers that be are ordained of God. Whosoever resisteth the power, resisteth the ordinance of God . . . For this cause pay ye tribute also: for they are God's ministers, attending continually upon this very thing. Render therefore to all their dues: tribute to whom tribute is due; custom to whom custom; fear to whom fear; honor to whom honor" (Romans 13:1, 2, 6, 7, KJV).

Let's especially focus on verse 6, this time using the *New American Standard Bible*: " . . .pay taxes, for rulers are servants [ministers] of God." You say, "Oh no! They're not very godly." In many cases that is true. Nevertheless, God has designed human government to keep society together, to punish the evil and to support the good. In the sense that government leaders rule in the place of God through an institution of God called human government, they are His ministers.

When you pay your taxes, you are in the truest sense supporting the work of God. That may come as a shock, but it's true. You say, "Well, if I cheat a little on my taxes here and cheat a little there, I'll have more money for the Lord." No, you will be robbing the Lord. You will fall into the category of Malachi 3:10 by not paying your taxes.

Christians should be especially cooperative in this matter. We know the God who established and endorsed the authority of human government. Cheat the government and you just cheat yourself out of blessing; you are taking for yourself what actually belongs to God. As a Christian, you ought to figure out every way you can pay your taxes. (Frankly, I have mixed emotions on this, but Scripture is clear.)

Pay your taxes (required giving), and God will bless you because you've been obedient to His principle and have supported His ministry. When we pay our taxes, we are funding a national entity which God has designed and over which God is sovereign.

Freewill giving in the New Testament. What about freewill giving? If the New Testament doesn't teach us to tithe, what does it say? How do we give? The Bible presents ten principles for our giving. If we're going to be serious about being good stewards with the money God has entrusted to us, and about being godly givers, we must know and practice these principles.

1. Giving is investing with God. "Give, and it will be given to you; good measure, pressed down, shaken together, running over, they will pour into your lap. For whatever measure you deal out to others, it will be dealt to you in return" (Luke 6:38, NASB). This

82

verse gives the *only* requirement connected with freewill giving: "give!" There is no mention of specific quantity or percentage.

This is the principle of investment. "Give and it will be given to you." How does God give back to you? "Pressed down, shaken together, running over." God's goods are not like those boxes of crackers or cookies that seem full at the store, but opening the box at home you find much less than you expected. When God gives back to you, His blessings are jam-packed and pressed together. In fact, you usually get more than you thought you would.

When you invest with God, you get a return that will last eternally. The realization of this should inspire great generosity.

Perhaps you've read the story of C. T. Studd, one of England's greatest athletes in the 1800s. Studd was a world champion cricket player who came to Christ. When Studd's father died, Studd inherited 29,000 pounds (probably worth $150,000 or more at that time). This was a sizable fortune in those days.

But Studd said, "I don't want that money to clutter up my life. I think the best way to use it is to invest it with God." He sent 5,000 pounds to Hudson Taylor, 5,000 to William Booth of Salvation Army fame, and 5,000 to D. L. Moody to start a work in India. Moody didn't go to India, but the money helped start Moody Bible Institute in Chicago. Studd gave other gifts to various servants of God, until he had only 3,400 pounds left. This he gave to his wife on their wedding day. But she said, "The rich young ruler was asked to give all." So they sent all remaining funds anonymously to General Booth. All of it. Then Studd said, "Now we're in the proud position to say, 'Silver and gold have I none.'"

The Studds invested every dime with God and then went to Africa as missionaries. Soon God's dividends started coming in, and they're still coming in today, all because that man was willing to invest his money with God.

C. T. Studd saw the truth of Matthew 6:19-21: "Lay up not for yourselves treasures upon earth, where moth and rust doth corrupt, and where thieves break through and steal: But lay up for yourselves treasures in heaven, where neither moth nor rust doth corrupt, and where thieves do not break through nor steal: For where your treasure is, there will your heart be also" (KJV).

Be sure that you invest with God,

because wherever you put your treasure, that's where you're going to put your heart. Let's say that I have $20,000 on hand. I could put my $20,000 into an earthly investment. You know what I would do then? I'd start thinking about that $20,000. Every time I get the paper I'd check on how my stock is doing. Before long, that $20,000 would start running my mind. I'd plug in to what's happening economically and start biting my financial fingernails. I'd worry about my investment. My attitudes and actions and responses would be toward the world, because that's where I put my money, and that's where my heart would be.

Let's say I take the same $20,000 and give it to God. Now what happens to me? I'm going to say, "Lord, use that $20,000 I gave You. I look forward to a return on it." This would deepen my relationship to Him. That's what Jesus meant when He said that where your treasure is, that's where your heart is going to be. Wherever your investment is, you are going to be preoccupied with wanting to see the dividends on your investment. So lay up treasure in heaven.

The main point is in verse 24: "No man can serve two masters: for either he will hate one, and love the other;

or else he will hold to the one, and despise the other. Ye cannot serve God and mammon." It's one or the other. If you would learn to invest with God, you would find yourself more in touch with God. You would be checking on your investment. I would much rather give my money to God than to any financial organization I know, wouldn't you? I don't care how many billions the savings and loan has. I want to invest as God directs.

Let's run verse by verse through 2 Corinthians 9, a remarkable piece of literature on giving to God.

Verse 6 tells us, "He which soweth sparingly shall reap also sparingly, and he which soweth bountifully shall reap also bountifully" (KJV). This is the key (cf. Proverbs 3:9, 10 and 11:24, 25). Paul gave a beautiful example of bountiful sowing in the previous chapter when he said of the Macedonian churches, "in a great trial of affliction, the abundance of their joy and their deep poverty abounded unto the riches of their liberality" (v. 2).

Someone says, "Pastor, how much should I give?" How much do you want? If you want to sow sparingly, that's what you're going to reap. Throw a token at God, that's what you'll get back. "Every man according as he purposeth in his heart, so let him give; not grudgingly, or of necessity: for God loveth a cheerful giver" (v. 7, KJV). Don't give out of compulsion. If it comes to that, keep your money — God doesn't need it. God loves a cheerful giver.

And as we give to Him, He gives it back. "God is able to make all grace abound toward you; that ye, always having all sufficiency in all things, may abound to every good work" (v. 8, KJV). You say, "Well, if I invest so much with God, I may run a little short. Sure, I'll get all spiritual blessings, and a bunch of people will get saved, and my Sunday school class will grow. But I'll have to buy an old Volkswagen. How much am I going to feed my family on spiritual blessings?"

Verse 10 was written just for you: "Now he that ministereth seed to the sower both minister bread for your food, and multiply your seed sown, and increase the fruits of your righteousness" (KJV). There are physical blessings and spiritual blessings. You get both. Listen to verse 11: "Being enriched in every thing to all bountifulness." Why? "Which causeth through us thanksgiving to God. For the administration of this service not only supplieth the want [need] of the saints, but is abundant also by many thanksgivings unto God." God wants your thanks, and God knows you'll thank Him if He keeps His promise and returns dividends. Do you think He will? Do you think God wants glory? If He gets it from thanks, do you think He will encourage you to have a thankful heart? He says, "If you'll invest with Me, I'll pour it back so you can thank Me and give Me glory." Believe Him; He'll do it.

In Matthew 19:21, Jesus told the rich young ruler to sell all he had, give it to the poor, then come to Jesus. Does this mean you have to give your money away to be a Christian? I don't think so. But Jesus was saying that your money can stand between you and Him.

There was once a slave who was a tremendous Christian and often told his master about the Lord. His master came to him one day and said, "You know, whatever you've got, I want it. You have such peace and joy and contentment, I can't believe it. How can I get this?" The slave said, "Go to the house, put on your white suit, and come down here and work in the mud with us slaves. Then you'll have it."

The master answered, "I could never do that. I'm the master, you're the slave. That's beneath my dignity." He came back a couple of months later and said, "I can't resist asking you again. What is it you have and how can I have it?" The slave repeated, "Go put your white suit on, come down and work in the mud with us, and you will have it." The master was furious and walked off. Finally, in desperation he came to the slave again and said, "I don't care what it takes. I'll do anything." The slave said, "Go put on your white suit and work in the mud. Will you do that?" "Yes," the master agreed. The slave said, "Then you don't have to."

Do you see the point? That slave knew what was standing between his master and Christ — pride, self. And he put the issue right out in the open. That's all Jesus was saying. Until you're willing to give up your money, you're separated from God. You can't serve both. You must be totally willing to freely, generously invest with God and wait for His promised return.

2. Giving is to be sacrificial. Mark 12:41-44 provides a beautiful example of this: "And Jesus sat over against the treasury, and beheld how the people cast money into the treasury: and many that were rich cast in much. And there came a certain poor widow, and she threw in two mites, which make a farthing. And he called unto him his disciples, and saith unto them, Verily I say unto you, That this poor widow hath cast more in, than all they which have cast into the treasury: For all they did cast in of their abundance; but she of her want did cast in all that she had, even all her living" (KJV).

Jesus was sitting in the court of the women, the Temple treasury, watching everybody put in their gifts. "Sat" and "beheld" were imperfect verbs in the Greek, which means Jesus continued to sit there and continued to behold. He watched the rich people come and fill the thirteen trumpet-shaped receptacles on the wall. And he saw the widow put in her tiny offering.

A mite was an eighth of a cent, the smallest coin of the day. She gave a whole fourth of a cent! That wasn't enough to buy lunch for a priest. What good was that going to do anybody? Yet Jesus saw in this incident a chance to teach His disciples. He taught directly from the living illustrations of life.

One of the principles I've learned about discipling people is this: discipleship occurs best in the application of the principles of truth to the living of life. In other words, to gather a bunch of people in a room and try to disciple them doesn't work. What you've really got to do is to apply biblical wisdom to the flow of life.

This is what Jesus did with His disciples. They walked through the world and He taught them from what He saw happening. He solved their problems with spiritual solutions. That's discipling.

So He called His disciples and commended the widow because she put in "more" than all the others. She had only a quarter of a cent left and she gave it. She gave everything she had, and you can't give any more than that.

The point Jesus was making was that sacrifice is the essence of giving. And the ultimate sacrifice would be to give everything. The least money was the greatest gift.

What does this teach about giving? Does this teach us to tithe? No. It teaches us to sacrifice, perhaps even giving everything we have. "But to do good and to communicate [share] forget not: for with such sacrifices God is well pleased" (Hebrews 13:16, KJV). What pleases God in giving is sacrifice. That has nothing to do with a tenth.

Paul, thankful for money he had received from the Philippians, wrote, "I have all, and abound: I am full, having received of Epaphroditus the things which were sent from you, an odor of a sweet smell, a sacrifice ac-

ceptable, well-pleasing to God." In return, "my God shall supply all your
need according to his riches" (Philippians 4:18, 19, KJV). You gave sacrificially, you invested with God. Now
He'll supply all your needs according
to His riches.

Giving is to be sacrificial. David
said, "I will not give the Lord that
which cost me nothing." Isn't that
beautiful? What a mockery it would be
to do that to Him. God isn't concerned about how much we give, but
about what it costs us to give it. Tithing would be for most of us far short
of sacrifice.

*3. Giving is not only a matter of what
we have.* People always say, "If only I
had more, I would give more." Really?
A preacher came to see a farmer and
asked him, "If you had $200, would
you give 100 of it to the Lord?" "I
would." "If you had two cows, would
you give one of them to the Lord?"
"Sure." "If you had two pigs, would
you give one of them to the Lord?"
The farmer said, "Now that isn't fair.
You know I have two pigs."

We've all done that, haven't we? If
only I had more . . . I wish I could
give more. Luke 16:10 has something
to say about this: "He that is faithful
in that which is least is faithful also in

much: and he that is unjust in the least is unjust also in much" (KJV). If you aren't giving sacrificially with what you have, you wouldn't give sacrificially if you had more. How much you have has nothing to do with it.

The Christians in Macedonia gave sacrificially, although they were poor ("the riches of their liberality," 2 Corinthians 8:2, KJV). They didn't have much, but they gave liberally. And they first gave themselves to the Lord (v. 5). Giving is not a matter of what you have. It's a matter of the heart. It's a matter of the sacrifice that you desire to render toward God.

4. If you can't handle money, you can't handle spiritual riches either. Here is one of the most sobering statements on giving anywhere in Scripture: "If therefore ye have not been faithful in the unrighteous mammon, who will commit to your trust the true riches?" (Luke 16:11, KJV). If you can't handle money (earthly riches), do you think God will trust you with spiritual riches?

Giving and spiritual riches go hand in hand. Those of us in Christian service have seen many disasters in this area. "If ye have not been faithful in that which is another man's, who shall give you that which is your own?" (v.

12). Do you think God is going to put you in a position to have real spiritual responsibility for other souls when you can't handle dollars? Don't you believe it. If you can't handle money wisely, you'll never be given that greater trust.

Here's the idea: A father wants to find out whether his firstborn son, the heir to his estate, will manage the estate properly. So he gives him x number of dollars and then watches to see how the kid handles the money — not for the money's sake, but as a measure of the young man's character.

I know men personally, close friends, who have had to leave the ministry. God has totally removed all of their spiritual responsibility because they reached a point at which they could not handle money. This is serious business. How you handle money will determine the extent and power of your ministry.

5. *Giving amounts are personally determined.* Luke 19 gives one of the Bible's more humorous stories. "And Jesus entered and passed through Jericho. And, behold, there was a man named Zaccheus, which was the chief among the publicans." Being a tax collector was like the kiss of death — everybody avoided him. Of course, he was rich because he could exact any

amount of taxes that he wanted, well beyond what he was required to pass on to the Roman government.

Now he sought to see Jesus. He wanted to find out about this person he'd heard about. There was a big crowd, and he was short; so he ran and climbed up a sycamore tree. "And when Jesus came to the place, he looked up, and saw him, and said unto him, Zaccheus, make haste, and come down, for today I must abide at thy house. And he made haste," which may mean he jumped out of the tree, I don't know. He came down and "received him joyfully." Zaccheus couldn't believe it.

They went to Zaccheus' home and had a wonderful time. Zaccheus got straightened out spiritually and said unto the Lord, "Behold, the half of my goods I give to the poor." Did he give 10 percent? No. Zaccheus gave 50 percent, half of everything he had. Now Jesus could have said, "No, no, all we require in the system that we have is a tenth. You may keep the rest." But the Lord never restricted giving to a tenth. That would have robbed Zaccheus of blessing. Then Zaccheus went even further: "And if I have taken any thing from any man by false accusation, I'll restore him fourfold."

The point here is that giving is spontaneous, an act of love and gratitude, not of lawkeeping. Our example is Jesus Christ who gave Himself: "Though He was rich, yet for your sake He became poor, that you through His poverty might become rich" (2 Corinthians 8:9, NASB). There's the pattern. You're rich. Now become poor, so others can become rich.

The amount to be given is to be determined between you and God. The important thing is to have a willing heart.

6. *Giving is to be in response to need*. It is true that giving is to be spontaneous and voluntary, pouring out of a loving, thankful heart. But giving in the New Testament is also to be in response to need.

For example, Acts 2:44, 45 says of Christians at the time of Pentecost that they "had all things in common; and they began selling their property and possessions, and were sharing them all, as anyone might have need" (NASB). And in Chapter 4 they were selling land and giving the money to the apostles to distribute to the needy. Acts 11 says there was a famine in Judea, and the saints collected money for Paul to take to the needy people there. No particular percent was required. Each believer simply gave what he could to help meet the need. For over a year, Paul collected from Gentile churches an offering for the needy poor saints in Jerusalem.

If a man comes along with a need and you can help meet it, it is your Christian responsibility to do so. Give to the Lord out of the wellspring of joy and gratitude and love in your heart. But give to help fill specific needs too. The two go hand in hand very nicely.

7. *Giving is to demonstrate love, not law.* "I speak not by commandment, but by occasion of the forwardness of others, and to prove the sincerity of your love" (2 Corinthians 8:8, KJV). This is not a legal system. This is not a prescription for a percentage. Our giving shows our love for God.

Love is the foundation of giving. An example of this is found in Romans 15:25-27 (TLB): "I must go down to Jerusalem to take a gift to the Jewish Christians there. For you see, the Christians in Macedonia and I've taken up an offering for those in Jerusalem who are going through such hard times. They were very glad to do this, for they feel that they owe a real debt to the Jerusalem Christians. Why? Because the news about Christ came to these Gentiles from the church in Jerusalem. And since they received this wonderful spiritual gift of the Gospel from there, they feel that the least they can do in return is to give some material aid." That's love, not law.

Verse 12 of 2 Corinthians 8 (and remember, this chapter deals with giving) speaks about "a willing mind." "Every man according as he purposeth in his heart, so let him give" (2 Corinthians 9:7, KJV). Don't give grudgingly, out of necessity, but out of love. If you put a prescription on giving, you put yourself under a law and rob yourself (or others) of some of God's blessing.

8. *Giving is to be planned.* "Upon the first day of the week let every one of you lay by him in store, as God hath prospered him" (1 Corinthians 16:2, KJV). You say, "Well, I don't give money, I give my talent or time or thoughts and ideas." That's fine, but that doesn't replace your responsibility to give money.

The "store" is the church, so it may have a reservoir out of which to meet needs. This is not referring to some private account, as is clear in Paul's statement, "that there be no gatherings when I come." He wanted it all given to the church, "in store," when he arrived. But at any rate you are to resolve in your heart and then lay in store as God has prospered. That means proportionately, on a percentage basis, though obviously this varies from person to person, and from time to time for any one person.

We are all to give weekly — "Upon the first day of the week let every one of you . . ." — so churches will have money available to meet needs as they arise, rather than always pleading for special money for special offerings. A budget is an important step toward such stability.

Giving is to be done systematically, proportionately, faithfully, as you "purpose" in your heart. The Greek word translated "purpose" means "to choose beforehand." You are to plan, pray, prepare — and not to give haphazardly.

Once in a while someone in my church will come up and say, "I'd like to give a check to the church. This is my giving for the next six months." I respond, "Wait a minute. I appreciate your spirit, but let me share with you a truth. The Bible says you are to give once a week, every week." Why? Because you need to learn consciously the stewardship of your money every week of your life. This is a focus each one of us needs.

9. *Giving is to be generous.* The

Macedonian Christians were commended because "the abundance of their joy and their deep poverty abounded unto the riches of their liberality" (2 Corinthians 8:2, KJV).

These people were poor, but they gave generously. The words translated "bounty" and "bountifully" in 2 Corinthians 9:5, 6 (KJV) refer to liberality. Giving is to be generous and sacrificial. We are to "abound in this grace" (2 Corinthians 8:7, KJV).

10. Generous giving always results in God's blessing. Paul expressed his gratitude to the Philippians by saying, "I rejoiced in the Lord greatly, that now at the last your care of me hath flourished again . . . My God shall supply all your need according to his riches in glory by Christ Jesus" (Philippians 4:10, 19, KJV). Would, could God supply *all* their needs? Yes, all.

In 2 Corinthians 9:6 we read that if we sow bountifully, we will reap bountifully. Verse 10 adds that God will give you bread for food, will multiply your seed, and will increase your fruit of righteousness. Verse 11 goes even further: "being enriched in every thing to all bountifulness" (KJV).

These are the principles of giving found in the New Testament. No wonder our Lord Jesus said, as recorded in Acts 20:35, "It is more blessed to give than to receive" (KJV). The blessings that will inevitably result from practicing these principles will come to every faithful steward.

CONCLUSION

WE HAVE learned that our giving should be sympathetic, systematic, purposeful, weekly. And (this is a tough one) our giving should be sacrificial. People often ask me, "How much should I give?" I don't know how much *you* should give. That's between you and God. But remember, Zaccheus gave 50 percent for a starter. I don't think that's the norm. But I'll tell you one thing, it sure shoots holes in the 10 percent theory. I don't believe you'll find tithing in the New Testament.

The important thing is to give sacrificially. David said, "I will not offer burnt offerings to the Lord my God which cost me nothing" (2 Samuel 24:24, NASB). I love that statement.

Giving should also be secret and humble (see Matthew 6). The Pharisees loved to announce, "I'm giving this much," so everyone would know and be impressed. God says, "Be quiet and humble. Let your giving be between you and Me." That's the way to give. "Take heed that ye do not your alms before men, to be seen of them: otherwise ye have no reward of your Father which is in heaven" (Matthew 6:1, KJV). If you give to impress men, then you get their praise, not God's. "Therefore when thou doest thine alms, do not sound a trumpet before thee, as the hypocrites do in the synagogues and in the streets" (v. 2). Can you imagine that? "Hey, everybody! Look, I'm giving!" Why this display? "That they may have glory of men."

Jesus said, "But when thou doest alms, let not thy left hand know what thy right hand doeth: That thine alms may be in secret: and thy Father which seeth in secret himself shall reward thee openly" (vv. 3, 4).

I can't tell you how much to give, but if law required a 10 percent minimum, I would think that barely scratches the beginning of what grace deserves.

When you consider how much God has given to you, can you possibly set a limit on how much to give to Him? He has given spontaneously and totally, freewill giving at its absolute best. Dare you do less?